the immaculate conception
of the
blessed virgin dyke

Ellen Marie Bissert

*Cover photos: Fran Winant. Cover & design: Ellen
Marie Bissert. Production: Ellen Marie Bissert,
June Rook, and Judith Stivelband.*

*Grateful acknowledgment is made to the following
publications in which some of the poems in this
collection first appeared:*

Alkahest, Amazon Poetry, American Poetry Review,
Balaam's Ass, Big Mama Rag, Clown War, Dark Horse,
Earth's Daughters, Integrity, Lesbian Voices,
Light, New York Radical Feminist Newsletter, Nexus,
Oakland Review, Prairie Schooner, Promethean, South
and West, Sunbury, 13th Moon.

This book is dedicated to the women in my life who urged me to fight.

CONTENTS

Prologue

1. Poems to Myself

2. Padre Island

3. Outcomings

4. Woman to Woman

5. Lamentations

Epilogue

rologue

poetry poetry

i started writing poems
seriously
because god couldn't perform miracles
because i was told i looked like a stringbean
because my athlete father died before he trained me for the Olympics
because my tap-dancer stepfather thought i was too skinny to be a dancer
because Lochinvar on the 103 didn't invite me to the prom
because his highschool literary magazine published my suicidal poems
because my girlfriend & i listened to Chopin's Nocturnes
she wanted to be a pianist
& i wanted to talk with her abt Beauvoir at the boatyard
to hold her
all night
as she dances for the fat businessmen driveling in Vegas
i am still writing poems
to release us

1. Poems to Myself

solo

i go mute
in necessary nightmares
wires cross & snap abt heads
now
encrusts lice
now
pelts black beans
now
finds toes
their movement, grasp & separation to grounds
now
an animal fierce
& late

i cannot sleep

father
cemetery after cemetery i ride
your name to place unknown child to unseen man—
yes a shot blossomed in fragile hairs
& you left me with bandaids
by a courtyard window i twirl with red strings
& crinkle   as shadows cross
my mother's wash slaps its unction
& hey Mister   i bring you flowers
withered in my arms

mother
his pebble found too soon
you a womb & unexpected nursed me
wooden doll   snapped now
your love cannot smooth that thorn of me/this
you'll not remember nor break to kiss
mother   i have
an orphanage
where seeds collect in beds
& the sun falls

burning

mutilation

i am waiting
as wetness
birds fly thru
& pluck my hairs
i cannot find the window
i cannot close the window
its red string coiling into my neck
i am waiting by a window
broke
    open

breakdown

there is something funny
abt bleeding
        when you press
a black window pane
& whisper

belladonna

1.   i'm bringing it back again
the door is opened
i go in
i stand in
front of the mirror
doors are opened/are closed
& closed
again i watch the mirror
the thinness of ankles, arms
the muscles bunched in the thighs
i
slide down
press
my lower back
into the hardness of the high black table
its white butcher's paper with thin white lines
crinkles & sticks
i wait
in stirrup
as the florescent lights
with their blue angular specks
cut
the metal clamp is thrust penetrating cold
& open

2.   hungers swell in their secret pockets
they come apart
red & brown
drip from some edgeless table
i hold my pills
their powders & coatings melt in my hands
i know it all & must practice
again
the hungers swell & swell
moving me beyond
& down

red red & water

i watch the pool
for the fawn from the spring forest
there is rain
drops imprint their whorls into my face

i am water
i wear
the life of my own red moon
rising & ebbing the sullen tides of salt

they drip
like swords hung above my head
i cannot escape
the satellite pulling the water's song
into cycle

Satie

there is a window
opening
to a secret window
wind
from rain blows thru
tender
& clear   a pear
sits
on the innermost ledge

ripens

menses as muse

1st day

menstrual blood smells salty & salt reminds me of cheese
that is why i'm eating 2 frankfurters & a lot of sauerkraut
a girl i knew in analysis wouldn't sit with me in a cafeteria
now i like meunster cheese when i'm exhausted
grilled white cheese sandwiches make me think of masturbation
when you jack apart the 2 pieces
the melted cheese comes off

2nd day

i've been reading too much & sleeping too little
today is the usual day
of small unhappinesses & bloated hungers
of suicidal women too intelligent
to live
yesterday i had my hair cut & i cried all night
the hairdresser believed he was an *artiste*
i wish i could believe i was an artist
it's november
& i just ate 7 grilled cheese sandwiches
i was thinking of dada
of the conversation i had with 2 dancers
of the boy who threatened to bite me
of the girl with the white insignia i wanted to touch
nevertheless
i was hearing Satie's piano music
i was feeling i wanted to move like a 23rd-century bell
down the hill of my street
hear me hear me
my heart sings Erik Satie
i am a hermit i am a hermit
i'm the termite at my mother's heart
officially
i've given up poetry
i go to dance concerts
that's why i was thinking of dada
at last night's opening performance i asked a pompous question
where are Merce Cunningham's dances coming from
the dancers said dada
without a doubt i'm a person who is self-indulgent
my life has been the derivation of some excess
what i meant was deprivation
i was thinking
of MOMA's dada exhibition i went to when i was having a crash

my girlfriend & i had camembert cheese & saltines
& went home & had each other
that's an oversimplification
friends/fiends
we went home & i played records & broke records
played records & read poetry
read poetry
& destroyed my poetry
finally
i had to ask her to leave
it was 4 o'clock in the morning
i lit an 8" red Moroccan cigarette & went to sleep
i'm not much of a poet
i confess
i failed to graduate with honors in poetry
nevertheless
my mentor supreme smiled
it proved an indication
i'm beginning to feel good i'm not a poet
my life is simpler
my life is a simple excess
i go to work type
write letters
type
were i a man i'd screw WACs & designers of jockstraps
but i'm not a man
today i am depressed
i am writing a story abt my life 2 or 3 years ago
it bores me
being a victim
of myself
of my sex
of my analyst who was an ugly nut
the effortlessness of certain types of beauty makes me cry
i bite
i will bite you if you can't cry
i am not normal
i'm sane

3rd day

looking over all of this
i think of having yogurt
this is not a fruitful association
i'll think of having strawberries
a lover i fed strawberry yogurt to
no a different lover c. 1969 was feeding me cherries
i wrote a poem abt that
but today the flow has stopped
& i have nothing
to say

17

2. Madre Island

care

on cool watered rocks
we opened in a feast
cherries & darkest tea
creating some new sun

to try the game
i threw the blackened teapot
away but
stained fingers
kept the lid
& filled some secret pocket

geometry

i continue to trace your heart
as if i were discovering your body in my head
there is no beginning
i am in a circle
tangent
but diameter
to an imaginary circle
whose pieces i cannot bring
together they are mine
floating within the circumference of a cloud
where i evaluate the atmosphere with only the tips of my fingers
which remember
you
are as spring water trickling thru
the softness in the undersides of your limbs
locking me
telling me to be free
now
as before
your smile washes over me like waves
telling me
come
& go
& come again

red

i've become numb with loathing
3 choices
rage, suicide & madness
they embrace
totally
the generalization of rape
say what you will
you do it & won't stop
the love you give is as small as cherries
each one a pit in my mouth
i press myself into the gray chips of a cold enamel table
i am relieved to be left alone
i tell you
go
this love
is a post for wiping
that brown shredding barber's strap
i'm not a butterfly to be caught
& slid behind glass
i'm flying
to get the nectar
before the rose petals tremble
& fall

married lovers

this has been going on intermittently
continuously & on occasion
3 years, 1 year & 5

a harvard lawyer
a catholic-school teacher of adolescent boys
a doctoral student who dreams of working with blind girls

his mother is a shrink
a pianist
a decorator

his father a judge
a businessman
his father is dead

his wife is a dancer
a home economist
she is an editor & studies psychology

thus he is happy mostly
& bored
mostly bored but very happy

this is where i come in
armed with only
my poems

he is a success
he cheats
& wins

he is afraid
he comes too soon
or not at all

of course
he is ever willing
but barely able

i am not innocent, beautiful
or stupid
it is my fault

that he wilts in my beautiful blood
that he can't dump his prick
unless he can ruin my life

this is his game
& he'll beat me if he's the loser

Padre Island

if i weren't lonely
i could not come to the window
i would not wait for the water to fall
birds refuse my bread
i need to capture the first feather of morning
before light measures my face

1. causeway

the dizziness has started
it's a rule
i march on
as the waters pull
i remain in attitude

how to be in air
as the hip
dives at the white line
which knows to hide itself

i am my crab
certain in my limits
scuttling as you bask
in the sun on the warm stones
by the waters

2. the crab moves sideways without turning

i used it several times while packing
BOGUS USED CARS   you repeated that
i watch the signs
                how manic
the cactus by the roadside
as you sped to the wild flowers past the palms
into the desert

i came for this
experiment of syntax
moving toward the crab hole
                i frightened
the crab to run to its death in the kidney-shaped pool
as i went to unravel
the faint salt lines on the shore

3. victors

my bed contracts
i can't breathe without light
i rehearse bed to window/window to bed
the sweeping out & piling in of sand in the corners
morality comes in ritual   to hoard
the white froth of terror from the cannibal crabs
we chased them into each other's holes
& waited

4.   photography

love is a vacuum
i've my own from a past
i can't want any pictures
i demanded
            concentration
holding the head beneath water
to photograph a pose
i examine now for care

5.   interior

you told the end at the beginning
the woman who ran out crying
she'd lost her identity
                  you said
you shuddered at the softness in my face asleep
it embarrassed
those bones which hide/hoard
pain beneath my face
                  i thought
i'd put up with you until you'd go
calculating for the peace
to redeem myself

6. lover

i ask what is sorry
as i wait in the tunnel
as i watch sparks cross my bitten toes
green
i see the lights that drive ahead
green
i repeat
i am not sorry
i am not a lover
i'm not
        i am
onto you
            you say
love is
i doubt
beyond scent
upon scent
alone

7. i remember i was lonely

i want to remember everything now that i'm alone
i want to be alone
that is why i remember everything
is nothing   i note
the raining of air-conditioners
the oblique sun shining boldly in its small deep sky
i finger the days
like long black beads
their flat morning sun burning
a fiery piston forging a bulb to contain me
this was the encirclement
breaking the needle's eye
aiming the needle at the heart
that waited until the moon was over to begin again
i remember
you as the phantom father
as i awoke practicing to recall nothing but
ebbing water

vernal

it's spring & all
my friends are rubbing up against each other like cats
former lovers are phoning for a lay
they haven't heard
or can't believe i found them all inept & unattractive
god can't help
the penis is dead
i have no envy
i insist on the elegance of flaming cores of flowers
on sleeping with someone who can at least dance with me
i'm shooting for my sanity
it's a piece of fake swiss cheese
i've been gunning

3. Outcomings

beyond the beat

finally
i'm ready for the *barre*
for the thin dark mistress
who strips me & exits
so amused
      i'm tucked beneath a stark room
with its green edge
          hunger presses
    into cells
    where someone twists
with the dark

Outcomings: 13 in 13

1. cherub

words come as dreams
in flight
they ride up as effervescence
& i need a new poetry
for you
your skin
i inhale again
again
your hair
an étude on inner sides
sinks
thru the blue air
into mine

2. new

what kind of poem
do i write
now that i've told you
i love you
i refuse an image
this is it   you are a woman
as i
no metaphors can i use
to disguise this
i tell you here
as you sleep tonight alone
love
i cannot but do

3. groves I

i must insist on speaking to you
my voice is gone
i've always needed silence
& can't remember how
but your eyes
as in the dreams
where i find myself outstretched
& defiled
sleeping in a compartment of a fast-moving train
and know it's this/this one i must keep
but am held back
& taken away
again

4. groves II

i called you
because i became frightened
& needed you
to dance with me
to press like flower petals the tiny bones of your back with my palms
tonight
i know you are sleeping with her
& wonder if she could hold you as tightly against the hardness
of still white stars
as i
who cannot be jealous
but for the full moon & the long night
i have to share

5. descent

it's my oldest poem
i can't sleep until i've decided
to leave   tonight
as i wait beside my window
ice drips
slowly   i beg
the song of your skin in my hand
& must leave
will leave/have left
the smell of Circe's song
pulling me down
down & in
to your deep brown hair

6.   note

how could i care
i know only disappointments
growing hard
like skin on my feet
this is what my poems were abt
now i'm mad with tears
i intone your name
wanting you to call
wanting your smell in my hands
i arrange your clothes
place them on my body
this is obscene
i have not changed

7. disappearances

i will control myself
after all
        these years
i know suicide
is cheap & easy
        to cope
i'll learn to disappear
ride the ferry
walk the Verrazano-Narrows Bridge
smack my face into a wall
smile
waiting for you to call & say
goodnight

8. valentine

romance is a fraud
i stole from a bakery to make me normal, sick & fat
it has nothing to do with puritanism
but valentine's a shitty night when after all my poems
you'll be sleeping with someone new
or someone newer yet
forget it   i feel reassured
at least this year i'll have to be a poet
i can't afford dancing lessons to save me from jumping off my roof
where i yell   *this is love why don't you believe me*
to some stern self hanging white sheets outside my bedroom window
there's no excuse for any excuse
i'm sick of living for flowers

9.   the return

i've come to take you to an exhibition
you're an artist

a box of paints dries by your bed
you drink

i sit on your yellow striped spread eating a banana
we smile

you drink
pull your cat's tail

a barometer hangs like a blue breast from a wall
there's a compass

a pair of pliers
still

i love you
love you

you love me
i pull off my shoes

i examine the 2 red holes in your black thumbnail
you remove your socks

a crest of moon is rising in the dark
no sky

Billie Holiday sings
Solitude

it is spring
& you make telephone calls

to the first to the second
i was the third

10. collection

a former lover yesterday
a new one tonight

here Billie Holiday sings
Solitude

i have your red thermos
your white wool socks

a black turtleneck with your perfume
i can't fuck you out of my heart

each one
litters this abyss like cars upturned

& smashed
i leave them as i left you

trembling
i call

to talk abt poems
to confess

i love you
it's spring

& you now love her
the one you told to go while i waited

staring into a streetlight
that night

i left
to carry your photo

to pick up with anyone
who wants me

11. another

you are a woman
i have no defenses in love against you
i cannot stop
i cannot love you less than myself
now as before someone calls
she is leaving you
i know
i know this despair
as sex burns love out
i hold you
loving the blood that drips like wine from our bodies
you kiss me hard
& go to her

12. reflex

my body opens like a hand
as i grope the dark for your breasts
i once held
kissing your neck

each day
now pours its rain into my bones

i feel the ache
naked

i am huddled to the edge of the bed
you are secret

i bring your skin to my face
my life with you is this

imagining

13. farewell

so what life is hard, bitter & sad
i can't make it my business
i'm not Sappho
i can't let the sun burn out my heart
i want to be alone & free
i want to be the girl dancing her life away on Bandstand
this week
i ached so dancing with the women i held in my arms
i could not write poems
now the days are long & the windows open
green rain rushes thru
wet wind
why does the whiteness of my body still turn out to her

4. Woman to Woman

saving the waltz

Zelda
how can i be tightropewalking the corners of my life
weeping
thru the night for
you
you given the beauty
i wanted
for the pain
inflicted randomly
as proportions of muscle, bone & brain
Zelda
i want alley cats everywhere to cry all night for you
we've your kind of body
dripping away
Alabama Zelda Alabama
Zelda
we are frustrated ballerinas
our feet locked to the floor
our legs flailing one against the other
relevé
plié
relevé ever
the talisman is the *barre*
where the body floats out on its sweat to the image
in the dark mirror
small, brown & insignificant
flying thru dawn

sleep sleep

i understand the hunger
in your sleep
& envy your escape
often i begged you
to teach me how to survive
how to keep from breaking
you insisted
you needed to keep away
from my helix of fat, fatigue & hunger
where i watched you
whirling down
& tried still
that night
there was no way   you shouted
defrosting chopped livers by burning the carton in the pan
but out   thick
in smoke i couldn't see
that seconal sleep
hidden in your raveled sleeve

women of the mirror

you've been dead 3 months
2 days ago he told me

again i wake in a cold sweat
in the kitchen a glass breaks in my hand

i stare thru myself into the wall
outside my window

this is where we stood
women of the mirror

he locked you
& placed me beside

you pulled me against you
your hand slid down to reveal your breasts

& hit hard
you wanted to see if i'd want you

your hand slid down
you knew he'd fuck me

his hand slid down against your breasts
he wanted to know if i'd want you

your hands slid down
lips

opening to kiss his darvon
hands cool as

glass
they hold our breasts

tight
to the dark

tanglewood

i find a sadness the same
now
as 5 years ago
& again i play the records you bought me
treading them like paths worn thru a forest
Rachmaninoff's Etudes   Chopin's Preludes
Brahms' B-Flat Piano Concerto
& breathe the skin
that held me
only to be pushed
away   yet again
& again to approach that music
persistent as cycles of blood & breathing
needing silence to be heard
needing you to listen
needing you
we traveled to hear the birds
together
as in a wish
we walked & walked
to hear a bird sing with Brahms' cello
& journeyed
away

sharing

i have left you to him
you are a princess
living in a high-rise luxury tower
you have given up your allowance to declare you live with him
he who suggested our meeting
who sleeps with men
who has lived with you for 4 years
i did not care
you were a woman who wanted me reaching into her body
into the juices that slip like warm butter
thru   over again
i think of your revelation
your best friend who you slept with
your best friend who he sleeps with
your best friend who slept with both of you
i think of it
diving into the undertow
wanting to ride the foam breaking against my skin
i come up
sand sticking adhesively to my brain
i gasp on the 2nd revelation
the woman you met coming in with him
as you were going out to meet me
she has slept with you
he has slept with her
you tell me
she picks up women in women's bars
for her boyfriend to sleep with
again the number—3
2 women & a man
a man with 2 women
this liberal male fantasy
crawls up & down my mind like a roach
as i picture the erotic photos marking place in his sheet music
over again you are coming to me from him
diaphragm still in
i circle its rim with my tongue
disgusted that you use me the way he uses you
hating being used by him thru you
over & over
i dream of caressing your hair to glisten silvery on my fingers
of reaching for the juice of your leafy red fruit
of sucking the milk of your menses
you do not know
i dream of the night moist & green
of walking arm in arm with you
your hair flying against my face
their rage shooting like lightning
fear shimmering like slime in my head

it thundered as i slept beside you
where i was shown the dark red lining in the subway walls
& am lost
i dream of it
& the black middle-aged woman
staring at me as i danced with you
she is sitting smoking a cigarette
she is sitting sipping a watered drink
she sits alone
i did not care
you were a woman who wanted me
wanted me swimming far into her body
& tonight i return to that same bar
staring into faces for your eyes
watching women dance as your body crests
a wave against mine
my table cruel as sand
i sit alone
as you now lie beside him
i do not care
you were a woman who wanted me
you were a woman who wanted me reaching into her body
you are a woman i can share with no man

history

across the street from the Dyckman House
on Broadway
a Slovak woman sells hot dogs

she sits on a small white folding stool
in her flowered dress
under an orange & blue umbrella

it says hot dogs
hot dogs
& cold drinks

she doesn't understand
my bags of books
cottage cheese & diet sodas

she doesn't understand
i hate hot dogs
i want to bring her home

i want to talk with her
we can sit at my enamel-topped kitchen table
& eat pirogies & pea soup

pumpernickel bread & butter
& i won't get fat
i'll become small & strong like her

i'll braid my hair & wear a babushka on my head
we'll work in the sun
drink ginger ale & dance the polka under a red moon

she doesn't understand
i want to bring her home
i want to throw away America

i want to throw away America
who doesn't love my name or hers
or the wideness of our hips

she doesn't understand
i want to hear her speak to me in Slovak
i want to listen to my history

i want to hear

mother

today's was not the ordinary phone call
i flung at you the dirtiest word from any gutter
LESBIAN
you cannot understand how
it happened
your angelic stringbean girl of satin ribbons
making skirts for toni dolls
cartwheeling thru any livingroom
both ways
look ma, don't cry
i whispered to you
that morning as i sat by the window tearing at bandaids
he had come back
drunk
& beat you
22 years old with a 3-year-old daughter
married to a tubercular alcoholic
beating you
beating me
he left
shooting back like a bleeding snake to his family in Pennsylvania
what was the terribleness in the dark
that night as he grew
large & potent with rage corrosive as the liquor
swishing in his belly
all day he'd spit it up
warm, red mucus
his lungs punching back for him
every day
as he'd wake knocked-out in that boxing ring
his defeat rising red & thick
in his mouth
he swallowed hard
he was a man
this was the Navy
throwing him in the tubercular ward
releasing him
200% disabled
that was the cure
they told him
operated
& killed him
in his will i am called by a name other than my own
did you learn to love him
as i did the woman of gin-spiked breath
long for his body
like a thick blanket in the night
somewhere to rest yourself
swim effortlessly thru soft waters Float

did you cry
& let him go cool
& useless like a jar of bacon fat
into the ground
did you find it
in his death
did you find it
marrying again
marrying that man
whose knee i'd sit on
did you do it to make us
smile
always i fall backwards in my dreams
cheating on everyone
talking abt
the dirty jokes
the girlie pictures
the bathroom games
of his family praying before
& after
each day
each meal
they were not like my father's who had betrayed & punished you
so evil so evil
my mind kneeled on rice in the corner
holding itself on a mantel
like a clock
can you hear me
hold me
now
that i choose the sex you are
to love

5. Lamentations

inside out

i am lazy
i am angry

the plaster falls above my bed
alone

i wait
for the flower of my white mustard seed

my blown-out diaphragm hangs from a nail
the sign says

                    NO
                    COPE

i've bled on pills
bled on an IUD

bled loving a woman of thorns
it has come to this

my body responding to each hate
with a hurricane

it misses you
diligent

intently licking the heels of Dante, Shakespeare & Joyce
sucking off the vipers at your balls

this is not derivation
i must believe

you want me to learn
you want me to find the spine in my back

you say
i too can become an artist

i must risk my life
we fuck

it's my responsibility
before you leave

i'm running
into the soft arms of terror

that are mine

to the most beautiful woman at my highschool reunion

after 11 years
she is still as sleek as an unspayed siamese
charming everyone into her audience
she is a winner
rising to associate director of a department store
quitting to have 2 children
(1 for each of her husband's houses)
nothing has changed
she is still as leggy as a doe
her iris-blue eyes
her long smooth arms holding me in confidence
as she complains
motherhood hasn't done much
she's as flat as ever
glancing toward the table of husbands
i try to pick hers
nothing has changed
short smug & meaty
they are still the inert boys at the highschool dances
quietly pumping sperm into voluptuous moviestars
the way they force air into tires
she is a winner
moving beyond the mysteries of padded bras
still needing to offer herself like cut melon to the male eyes
opening her blouse
we will never be able
as i hold her cool thin fingers
i long to caress the silk of her nipples
into loving themselves
like the woman waiting for me tonight
does to mine

menstrual lamentation

every day
the story seems the same
every day
a wife is beaten like a dirty rug by her husband
every day
a woman is found headless
peeled down like a banana in her bedroom
every day
a woman is cut & scattered like litter in her apartment
every day
a woman is thrown in some alley
a broken coke bottle shoved up her vagina
every day
a woman dies in a tubular pregnancy with her IUD
every day
a woman is murdered by despair
every day
women's breasts, buttocks & legs are measured for a joke
they are hung to dangle
in men's minds like cuts of meat in a butcher's
women starve, shave & smile
anointing themselves
with the pearly whiteness that shoots
potent as money
they suck hard for it
& gag with pain
on gynecologists' tables
coldmetal caterpillars blooming into bats in their vaginas
these are the women
working with me in offices
in the supermarkets where i buy my food
measuring me against themselves
they will not know me
or even pity me as do my friends
their lovers installed
telling me my anger is a personal problem
as each day they sleep longer & feed
that depression growing fat like a fetus in their gut
they have no reason for madness
they are not me
whose lovers were irresponsible & impotent
whose lovers were brutal
whose lovers were skilled in the putdown
they are not me
who can love only women
but each month
women are secretly weeping
for all the ones we could not hold on to
slipping
smooth & silken out of our lives

the immaculate conception of the blessed virgin dyke

13th day

my qualifications are suspect
i am neither blessed nor virgin
i've slept with men
given that up
i've slept with women
not quite ditto
i am becoming an antique virgin
a virgin as in antiquity
like Artemis
like Sappho retired
i am in control
of myself
myself
i am in revolution
spinning like a propeller thru the clouds of paralysis
i am in revolution
I AM AT WORK
& finally working
not cleaning the house
or having sex
or sleeping
i am at work but waiting
ankles swollen
stomach bloated
i wear the punishments of oppression
i must be this body
back swaying out like a swing from my spine
fingers fat, fatter
my body waits
i grow globelike
eating pickles, cheese & bacon
i am now 13 days
late
this has never happened
it is only exactly the same
as last month
i wish it were a neurosis
to be picked away with rolls of money
where is the nearest doctor
so i can strangle him
he ignores & humiliates me
i am so tired of waiting for him
i want to remove the testicles of his mind
in the subway tunnels of 42nd Street & 8th Avenue

my dirty switchblade will ejaculate like a prick in his ear
he will learn to love it
he will learn women have work

the dream

i go to my doctor's
i wait
i go into his examining room
& remove his genitals
i give him the freedom he has longed for
his penis becomes erect
i wash & dry it off
i arrange the apparatus on my head
the penis because it is not a penis grows larger
it is a horn
i am a revolutionary unicorn
the medical profession pursues me for my powers
my body is firm
& glistening with magical salt
i am driven to a nearby hospital in a violet limousine
in an enormous room full of unicorns
Artemis anoints us with our sacred menstrual blood
& kisses our eyes

14th day

there was a solution to all this
a handful of diuretic & potassium pills
followed fast with ice water
i can sit at my desk & receive phone calls from my mother
yesterday
she returned my Amelia Earhart suitcase
& stole the poem in my typewriter
she cries now
that i am a writer
that i am a lesbian
that i am a lesbian who writes
what do my neighbors think
what do they say
a secretary where she works
lives in the apartment house next to mine
my mother sobs
because this woman has told their office abt my life
my mother sends me articles
abt VD, pornography & common sense from the *Reader's Digest*
my mother calls to ask if she is normal
she can't laugh with the women in her office who look at *Playboy*
& giggle all afternoon
nervously
she tells me they eye the younger women

the beauty of their bodies
the men in their boredom are attracted
the men in their insecurity are attracted
they choose them
then discard them like used paper cups

15th day

i call my doctor to ask
if i must have a period
since i can't have one
i don't want one
anymore
i'd rather have
the fantasy of Frye boots
today it comes
marching into my stomach
a giant army of porcupine paramecia
claustrophobic
they stand eating spaghetti with madness
like bristly gumdrops they tumble into my legs
i am transformed
into an everyday Amazon
shooting obnoxious men in the penis with my watergun
filled with menstrual blood
i roam city parks unharmed
rapists fall down
kiss my magical boots
& repent
i wander along Park Avenue
marking each doctor's door with the blood of slaughtered penises
our time is coming
our time is coming
but mine is not today
4 aspirins
2 darvons
1 heating pad
& bed rest
still the paramecia feast in the politics
of vengeance

16th day

it's all over
i am not pregnant
i am not menstruating
my body has given me this poem
while the moon of the new cycle spins
its revolution
my body is getting ready
getting ready
to give me another

the breast of june

i am working it out
lifting weights like mammoth butterflies in the air

it is a cold april morning
in my dark bedroom

on my radio Bach's Partitas for Unaccompanied Violin
i am dancing

to the strength of my lover's back
the muscles in her hands & thighs

unafraid of the mice in my kitchen
of the rat that runs the marathon inside my ceilings

it is the cruelest month the cruelest month
for my cruel mouth & unprotected heart

i wake dreaming of endless women poets flushed down
like bloody tampons

i wake plotting to stick splintery broomsticks
into the assholes of rapists

my mind is so refined
i string foreskins into Artemis' necklace

meeting june in march
this morning i want to twirl my tongue like a pinwheel in her ear

all day as the dogs in the next apartment die
howling on their lust

my mind is so refined
ascertaining the tenderness in my breast

i think of the breast of June
& our menstruations on the sheets

Epilogue

A Romance

romeo couldn't come
& god is a stupid ass with a limpleaking prick
that's why i need to be some poet
i never got invited to the prom
but got hot on Nothingness & did the polka with my dog
i blame my tubercular father who died before he could remember my name
my married lovers who could've loved me if i looked beautiful
& my monkey-faced analyst who needed me to be screwed
i don't give a shit if sperm freezes over
i'll die alone & dig it
loving a woman in a black leather jacket
& walking into The Duchess with my polka-dot tie & lace shirt
this is my life & i now ask everyone to dance